You Alone!

...Worthy of Our Praise

ARRANGED BY

JOHN DeVRIES

This special church musician resource, edited by Keith Christopher,
preserves the high energy of the studio recordings while adjusting vocal ranges
and voicings in consideration of a live worship presentation.
Studio instrumental charts have been adapted by Keith Christopher
and Dwayne Pedigo to conform to the Genevox Power Praise Band format.
The rhythm-based instrumental arrangements provide ample substitutions and cross cues.

Companion Products Available:

Listening Cassette 0-7673-3941-X
(Listening Cassettes available in quantities of ten or more for $3.00 each
from your Music Supplier or Genevox Music Group)

Listening CD 0-7673-9102-0

Accompaniment Cassette 0-7673-3942-8
(Side A Split-track; Side B Instruments only)

Accompaniment CD 0-7673-3943-6 (Split-track only)

(The studio vocals on the listening and accompaniment recordings
are fully compatible with the re-voicings found in this edition.)

Cassette Promo Pak 0-7673-3946-0

CD Promo Pak 0-7673-9103-9

POWER PRAISE BAND INSTRUMENTATION: Woodwind (Primarily an Alto Sax part, with passages
for Soprano Sax and Flute), Trumpet I, Trumpet 2 (or Alto Sax), Trombone 1 (or Tenor Sax), Rhythm,
Drum Set, Percussion
OPTIONAL PARTS: Flute (also includes Flute portion of Woodwind part) Trombone 2 (Baritone Sax),
Synthesizer (includes cues for all solo passages).

A fully-notated piano part is found in this choral edition.

GENEVOX

Code 0-7673-3940-1

FOREWORD

These are exciting days in worship. With the time-honored music of the past and the fresh, contemporary songs of today, we find a wealth of material from which meaningful services can be developed.

The newer material includes songs of great quality and character that may even become known as **classic.** As traditional music found its way from the hymnal into choral arrangements and beyond, so will this music find its place in worship, be it congregational, choral, or a mix of the two. The book you are holding contains such songs.

You may find much of this music appropriate for congregational use. If so, utilize your choir or ensemble to introduce the song in worship, then gradually let the congregation become part of singing it. Experiment – have fun as you discover, create, and lead your own version of blended worship.

Keith Christopher, *Project Coordinator*

CONTENTS

Come and Praise

Words and Music by
GARY MINK
Arranged by John DeVries

Tenor / Bass opt. until meas. 11

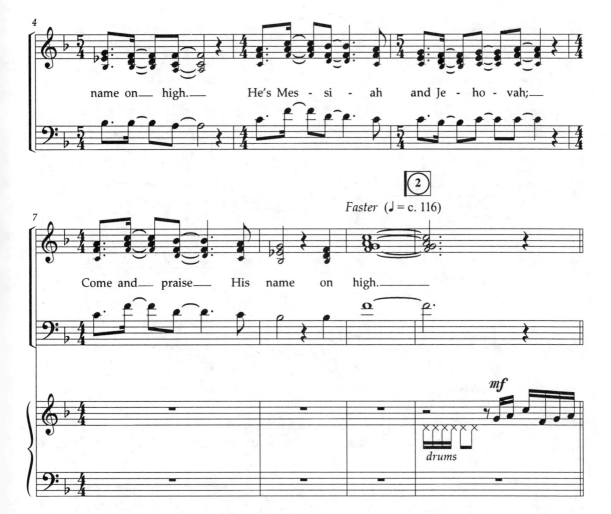

*Four clicks precede the vocal entrance on the split track.
The stereo tracks (instruments only) begin in meas. 10.

Come and— praise— His name on— high.—

Come and— praise—— the

Solo continues

Come On into the House

Words and Music by
JAY TURNER
Arranged by John Devries

Lord.

Come in - to the pres - ence of God,_____ our ho - ly Sav - ior;

Come on in and wor - ship with praise_____ in your mouth._____

r.h. optional to meas. 45

Be Ye Holy

Words and Music by PATRICE RISI
Arranged by John DeVries

ho - ly,_____ our God is ho - ly._

our God is ho - ly.

Our God is

Our God is ho -

ly,_____ ho - ly._____

O Give Thanks

Words and Music by
DANNY DAVIS
Arranged by John DeVries

*The cued ladies part may be substituted for the higher men's part.

thanks un-to the Lord, for He is good.

O give thanks un-to the Lord, for

He is good, for He is good.

Sing and Rejoice!

Words and Music by
JAY TURNER
Arranged by John DeVries

*Seven clicks precede the vocal entrance on the split track.
The stereo tracks (instruments only) begin in meas. 8.

Note: On the accompaniment track, drums segue this song immediately into "Your Love Lifted Me."

Your Love Lifted Me

Words and Music by
KEITH FERGUSON and BRUCE GREER
Arranged by John DeVries

*Basses may sing melody down an octave.

Whatever It Takes

Words and Music by
AARON TOMES
Arranged by John DeVries

60

With My Life

Words and Music by
MARK DEWBRE and MARK THOMAS
Arranged by John DeVries

*Meas. 6-26 may be performed as a trio. In any case, the lowest ladies part may be substituted for the higher men's part. The bass part (duplicating the melody) is optional meas. 6-26.

63

With my life I will praise— You; I will glo-ri-fy— Your name—

with each breath You give. With my life I will praise— You; I will

seek to hon - or You— with the way— I live, with my life.

You Alone Medley

Includes
You Alone Can Satisfy
What a Wonderful Lord
You Alone Are Worthy

Arranged by John DeVries

Relaxed (♩ = c. 64)

Solo (or S & T) *mf*
*You, Lord, sat-is-fy— my hun-ger;

CHOIR (or A & B) *mf*
You, Lord,

You, Lord, sat-is-fy— my thirst; You, Lord,

You, Lord, You, Lord,

74

Vocals continue a cappella
a tempo

You a-lone__ are wor-thy of our__ praise;__

F2
a tempo
let ring

You a-lone__ are wor-thy of our__ praise;__

Hymns of love__ and thanks to You we raise;__

slight rit.

You a-lone__ are wor-thy of our__ praise.__